FURNISHING THE HOME GROUNDS

A Canopied Double Seat That May be Used on Golf Courses, at Summer Cottages, in Parks, and on the Home Grounds

Furnishing the Home Grounds

By
KEN F. SHEPARDSON

THE BRUCE PUBLISHING COMPANY
MILWAUKEE

Copyright, 1936
The Bruce Publishing Co.
Printed in the U. S. A.
(Fifth Printing — 1942)

INTRODUCTION

Instructors, pupils, and home owners, at some time or other, desire to construct a piece of attractive lawn furniture, a decorative fence with an arched gate, a trellis, a swing, or a flower box in order to make the home grounds more enjoyable. It is the aim of this book to show how a number of these pieces can be made from standard-dimensioned softwood and with common tools.

Commercial designs of lawn and garden furniture are easily attainable, but all of them contain only very meager specifications. An experienced woodworker can reproduce them in a satisfactory manner, but the novice will find difficulty in making a sturdy and decorative piece from a mere pictorial illustration.

The drawings, eighteen in number, are made so as to allow a choice in design and construction. It is up to the builder to decide the kind and size of pieces which will best improve the home grounds.

It is suggested that the home grounds be plotted so that any future changes which may be made, such as the addition of outbuildings, the planting of trees and shrubs, filling or lowering the lot, etc., will not cause any difficulty. The beauty and durability of these pieces to be made will depend upon their appropriateness, construction, and finish.

As the drawings are quite detailed, only a brief description of the construction is given for each. It is taken for granted that the users of this booklet have had some experience in the handling of woodworking tools and the reading of drawings. The figuring of the bills of materials is left to the worker. It is suggested that sizes and grades of materials be compared and a full bill of material be made out before starting to build. It should be remembered that in the long run the poorer grades of lumber are not always the cheaper.

THE AUTHOR

CONTENTS

	PAGE
INTRODUCTION	5
MATERIALS AND FINISHING	9
LAWN BENCH	11
LAWN OR PORCH SET	13
CHILD'S CHAIR	15
LAWN SETTEES	17
LAWN OR PORCH SETTEES	19
LAWN OR PORCH CHAIRS AND SETTEES	21
LAWN OR PORCH TABLES	23
ARCHED GATES	25
ARCHES	27
FENCES	29
ARCHED GARDEN SEAT	31
TRELLISES	33
JUNIOR PERGOLA SWING	37
SENIOR PERGOLA SWING	39
SWING	41
CANOPIED DOUBLE SEAT	43
FLOWER BOXES	45

MATERIALS AND FINISHING

Because of its workability, strength, and weather-resisting properties, white pine is recommended as most suitable for the construction of lawn and garden furniture. Other kinds of wood may be used in some cases to advantage.

Finishing

Before painting, pitchy knots should be shellacked to insure against the pitch seeping through. White is always in good taste, but here also the builder must consider the surroundings. Three light coats of good exterior paint are better than two heavy coats. The first coat may be pure linseed oil. Some white lead may be added to it, especially if the succeeding coats are to be white. Boiled linseed oil dries faster than raw linseed oil, but either may be used. After the first coat, apply putty over any parts to be filled. Work the putty well into the crevices. Each coat of paint, except the last, should be sanded in order to insure a smoother final coat. The end grain should be allowed to soak up all the paint it will take.

Anchor posts and parts which are to fit below the ground line should be given a good coat of creosote to preserve the wood. The shingles on the double-canopied seat in Figure 17 preferably are stained green.

Fasteners

The cement-coated nail holds more firmly than the uncoated. Galvanized nails are weather resisting, but if the wood is kept painted they are of no particular advantage. Screws hold better than nails and are to be preferred where added strength is needed. In heavy construction, bolts and lag screws should be used.

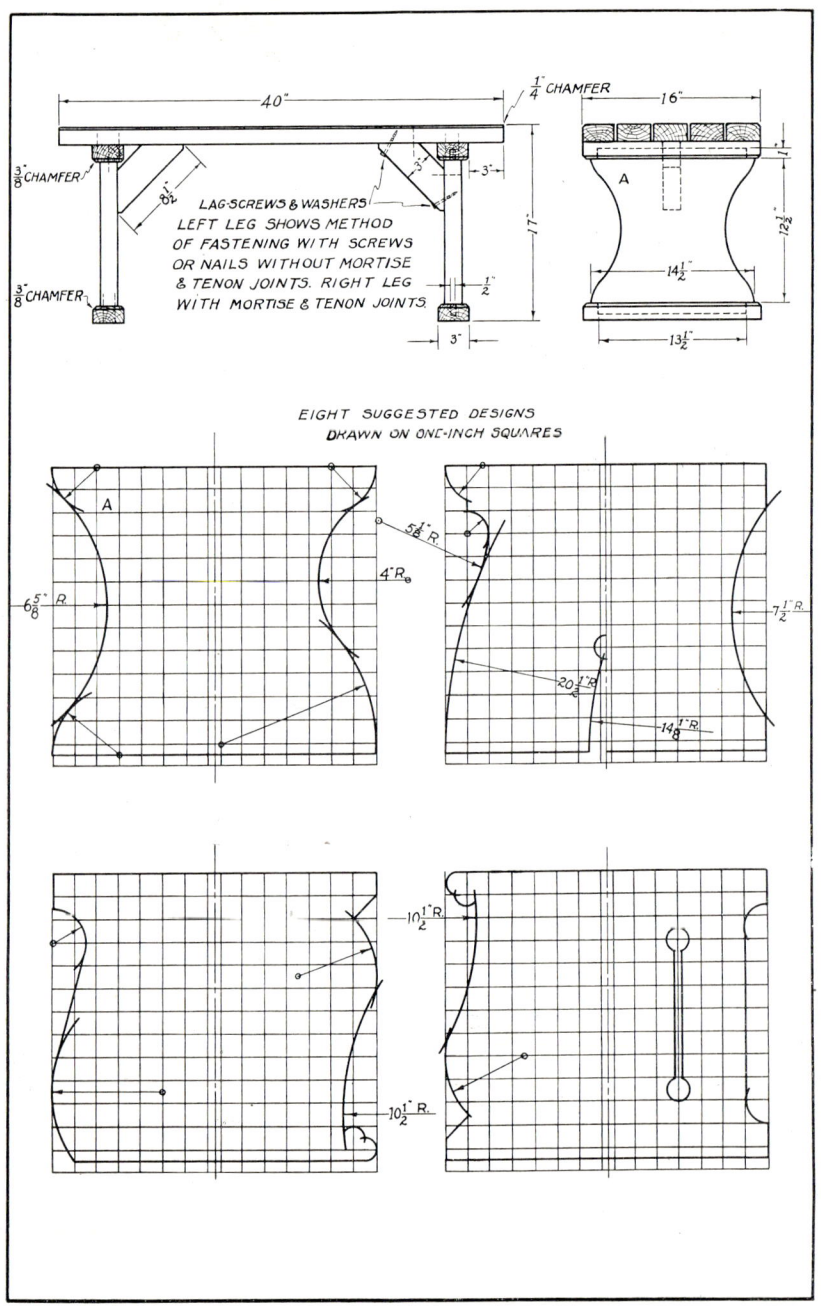

Fig. 1. Lawn Bench

LAWN BENCH

A lawn bench is appropriate and useful on all home grounds, and is very decorative if well designed and painted white.

Construction Details

The lawn bench is shown in Figure 1, together with eight suggested end designs. In choosing a design, place one hand over the part which you are not considering, in order to visualize the full pattern.

A Lawn Bench

End stock is glued up with casein waterproof glue and if mortise-and-tenon joints are not used, three $1\frac{1}{2}$ by 2-in. dowels should be inserted.

Divide a piece of stiff paper $7\frac{1}{4}$ by $12\frac{1}{2}$ in. into 1-in. squares, as illustrated. Don't forget to allow for mortise-and-tenon joints if they are to be used. Then the one-half pattern is laid in place and marked; reverse, and repeat the marking. If tenons are used, they should be marked and sawed before cutting out the ends according to design.

The other parts of the bench require no explanation. Before assembling, methods of fastening with nails or screws and the order in which this must be done should be studied. If mortise-

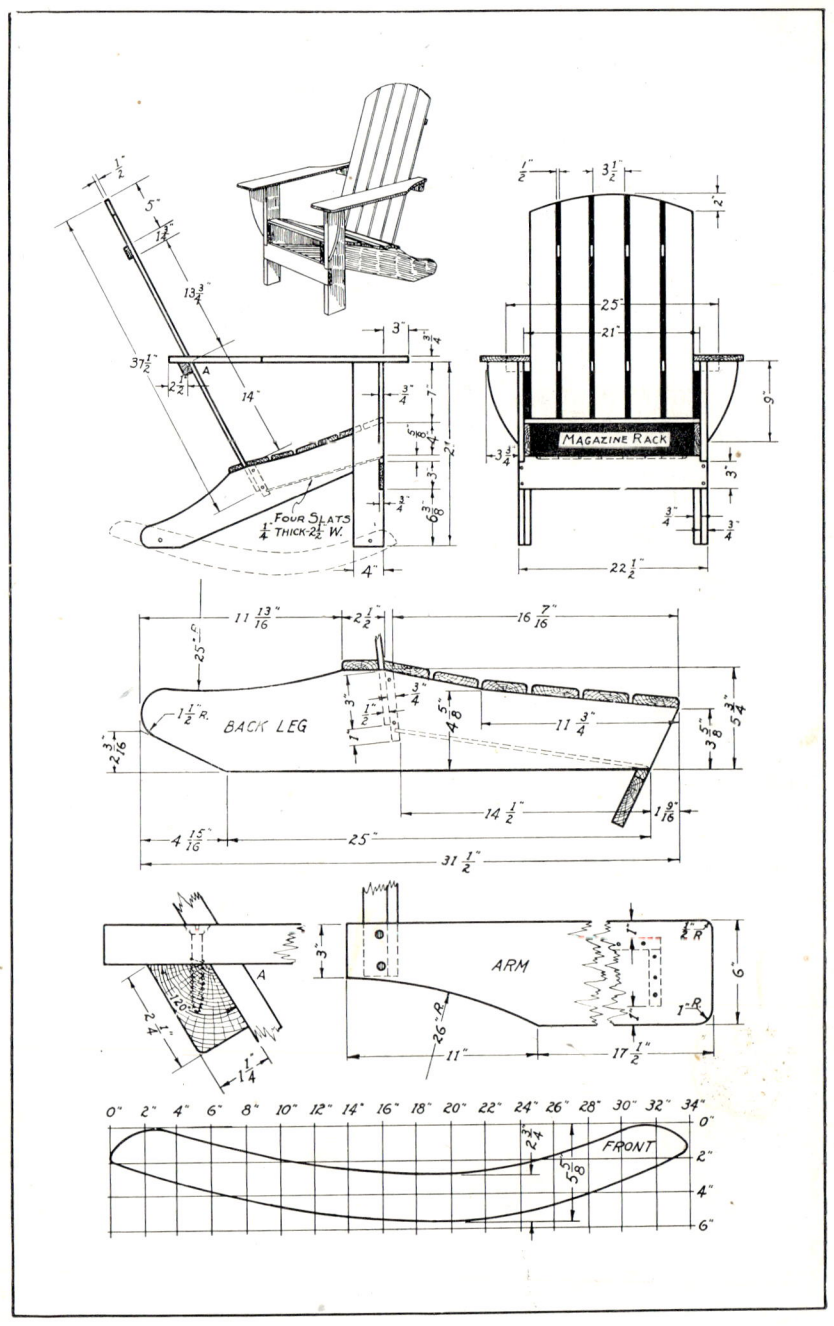

Fig. 2. Lawn or Porch Set

and-tenon joints are used, the upper crosspieces should be fastened to the underside of the seat slats before gluing the joints. Lag screws are used at an angle in order to strengthen the braces which have already been nailed in position.

LAWN OR PORCH SET

The lawn or porch set in Figure 2 is built for comfort and relaxation. A three-piece set, including a straight chair, a rocker, and a settee, forms an ideal combination. The settee seat should be twice as wide as the chair seat and constructed in the same manner, with the addition of a center brace placed between the seat and the magazine rack. For the rocking chair the only additional parts are the rockers and bolts for fastening.

Construction Details

All parts must be carefully measured because the slightest miscalculation will throw all related parts out of position. The arms are parallel to the ground and are fastened to the 120-degree brace piece with flat-headed screws as shown in Figure 2 at A. The back legs are fastened to the front legs from the inside by flat-headed screws.

Cement-coated nails are preferred wherever they can be used. They should be clinched about $\frac{1}{4}$ in. across the grain where they will show the least. Longer cement-coated nails should constitute the other fasteners.

After the back slats have been nailed into position, bend a yardstick to the desired curve and then draw the line; this is the easiest method of marking the curve. The top of the settee back may have one full curve or two curves each the width of the chair back. Designs may be cut in the wing arm supports and back slats (see Fig. 3).

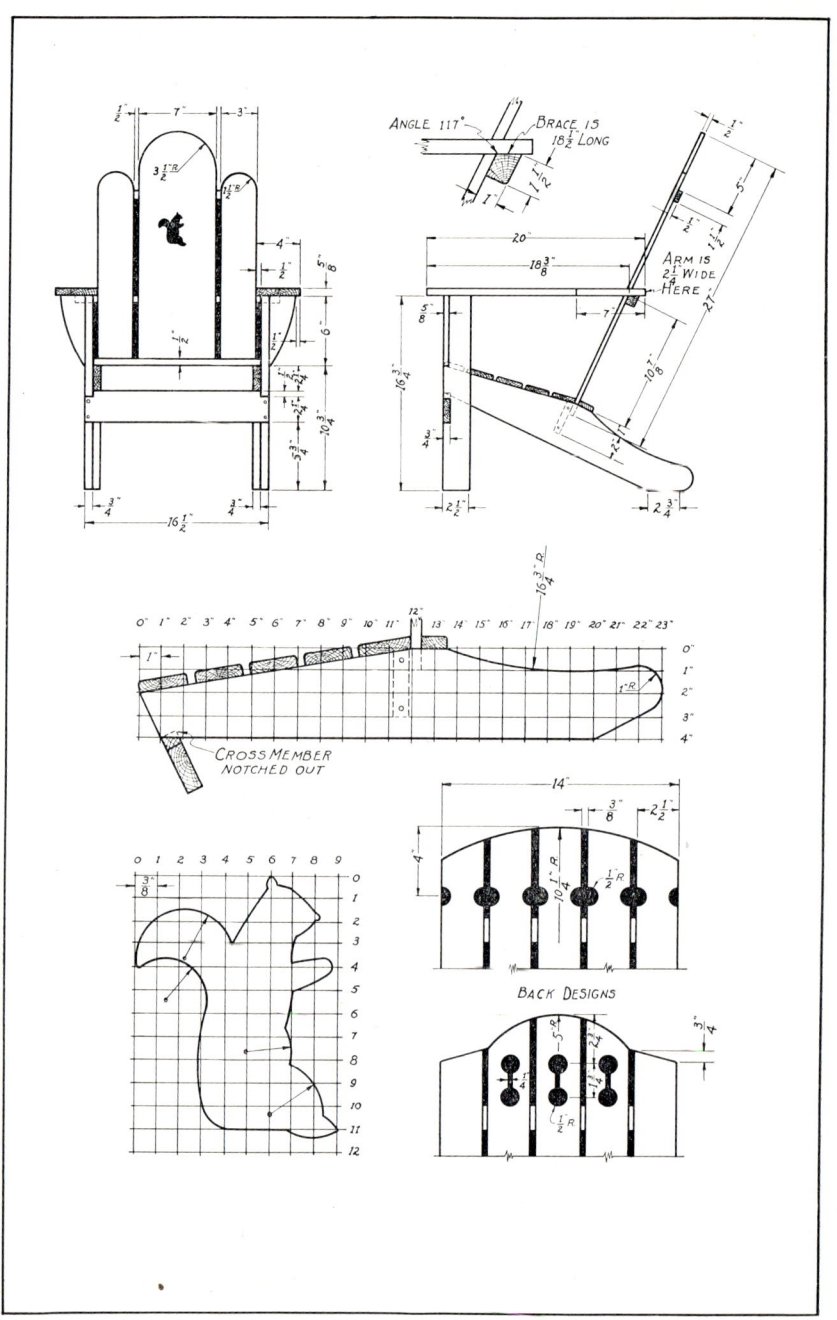

Fig. 3. Child's Chair

CHILD'S CHAIR

The size of this chair permits it to be used out of doors as well as in the child's playroom.

Construction Details

The chair is built in the same manner as the chair in Figure 2. The 18½-in. back brace is trimmed off at an angle of 117 degrees (see Fig. 3). The arms of the chair are parallel to the ground. The back of the arm tapers on the outside from 4 in. to a width of 2¼ in. The pattern for the back legs is drawn by the aid of 1-in. squares either directly on the wood or on the stiff paper and then transferred.

The squirrel design is drawn on stiff paper with the aid of 3/8-in. squares and a compass. The design may either be painted on in black or cut out with a coping saw. The squirrel may be transformed into a bear by omitting the tail.

The suggested back designs are easily made. In the upper design, two slats are placed together and a 1-in. hole bored at their intersection. In the lower design, 1-in. holes are bored. A coping saw is threaded into the top holes, and a portion between them and the lower holes is sawed out.

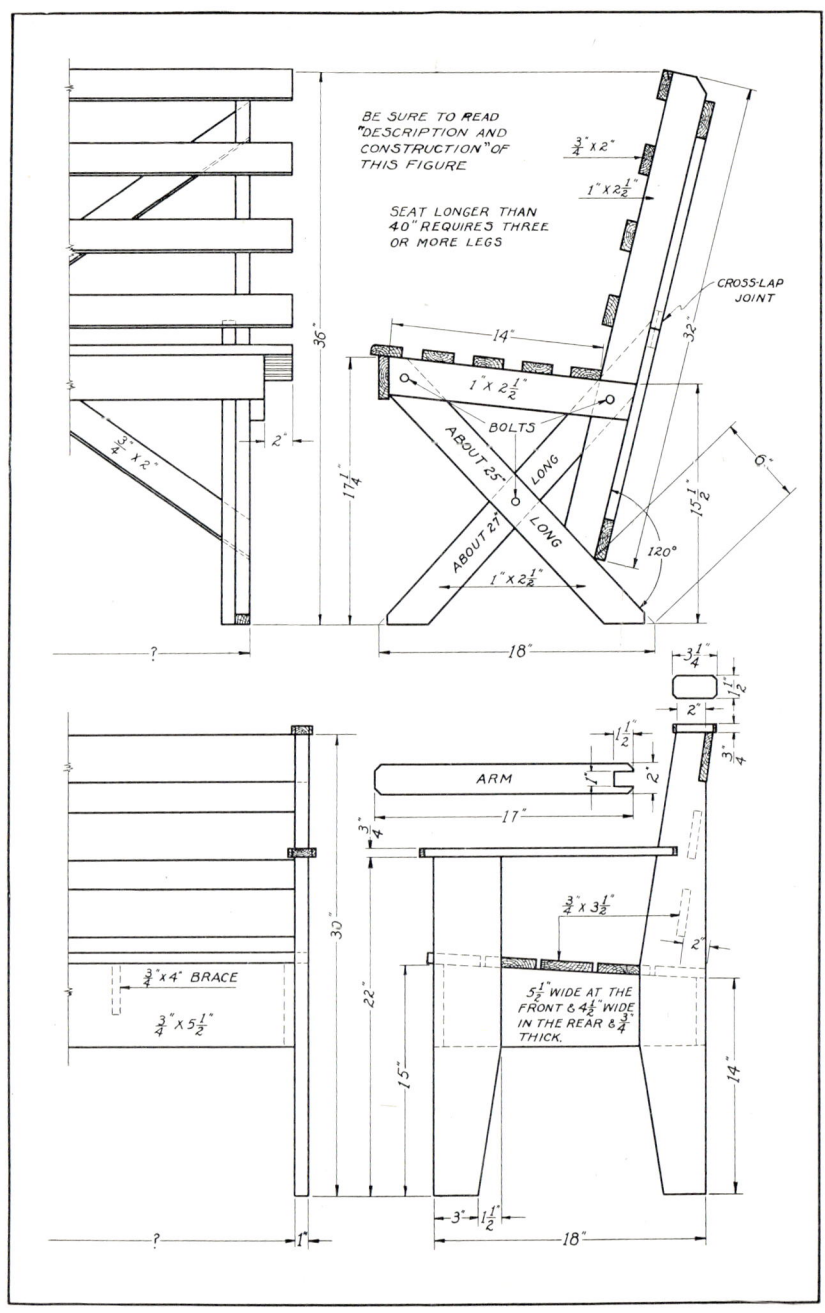

Fig. 4. Lawn Settees

LAWN SETTEES

These settees are very simple, yet serviceable and comfortable. No difficult joints are necessary. The builder can determine the length of the settee to suit his particular needs.

Construction Details

Two methods may be used in building the top settee. A full-sized drawing of the end view may be drawn on building paper and the parts assembled on it and lightly tacked together. The bolt holes are then bored. The bottom hole is 8 in. from the floor and 12 in. from the bottom of the legs before the toes are cut off.

The second method is to cut the four end pieces: 27, 25, 16½, and 32 in. The ends of each piece are squared. An acute angle of 60 degrees is then cut on the 32-in. piece. In the center of the 27- and 25-in. pieces (center of the width and 12 in. up from the bottom of each) an 8-penny nail is driven in three quarters of the way. The 60-degree angle is tacked to the 25-in. piece, 6 in. up as shown. Then the 27-in. piece is tacked to the 32-in. piece. A 1¾-in. wide straightedge is laid on the floor and the assembled parts are held in a vertical position next to the straightedge. The angles on the bottom of the 27- and 25-in. pieces are marked by drawing lines 1¾ in. from the floor, guided by the straightedge. The 16½-in. piece is tacked in position 15½ in. from the floor at the rear and 17¼ in. from the floor at the front. Finally the ends are completed by adding the holes and bolts and trimming off the projecting pieces. The front vertical cut may be marked by holding a 24-in. steel square on the floor alongside of the end held in a vertical position.

Usually if the seat bench is over 40 in. long, it will tend to sag. If this is the case, two pieces the same as the ends should be inserted, one 27 in. and the other 25 in.

The back braces are tacked into position and the cross-lap joint marked before the back slats are nailed fast. The cross-lap joint is to be cut out and braces are nailed into position. Then all projecting ends are trimmed off.

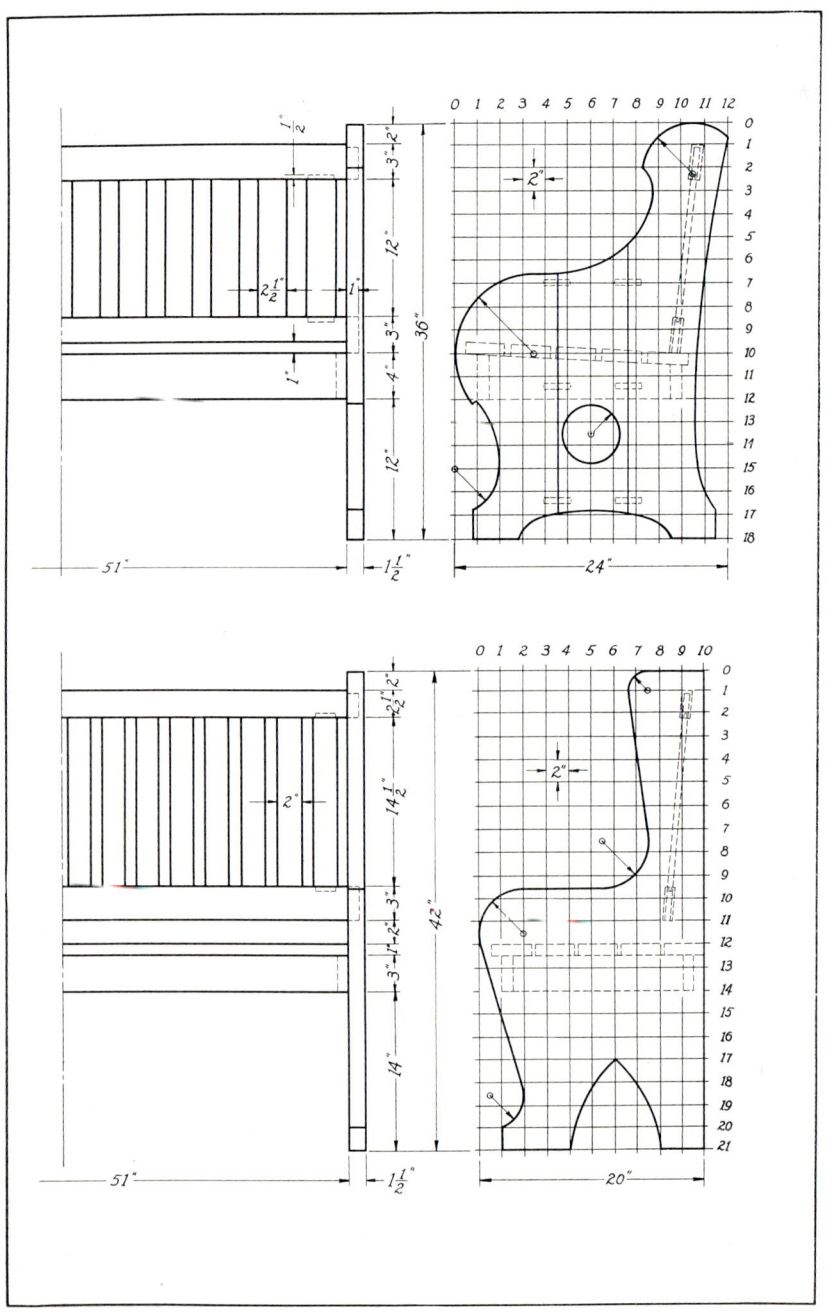

Fig. 5. Lawn or Porch Settees

The construction of the bottom settee can be figured out from the drawing itself. The legs are fastened to the end rails with nails clinched on the inside. If the length of the settee is over 60 in., seat braces should be added and back slats increased to 1 in.

LAWN OR PORCH SETTEES

When used on a porch these settees usually come in pairs (see illustration). They are of heavy construction and not so portable as the other settees in this book. They may be used for the lawn or garden although they are not so well adapted for this purpose because of the thickness of the end pieces.

Construction Details

The patterns are made with the aid of 2-in. squares drawn either directly on the glued-up ends or on heavy building paper and then transferred to the wood. The joints should be carefully made with three $\frac{1}{2}$-in. dowel pins $2\frac{1}{2}$ in. long at each joint and

Settees Used on a Porch Entrance

then glued; this will insure permanence. Casein waterproof glue should be used. The end pieces for the settee at the top in Figure 5 are made of three pieces each 8 in. wide. To save lumber, make one piece 36 in. long, one 26 in. long, and one 24 in. long. For the bottom settee in Figure 5 use three pieces, one 42 in. long and the other two 24 in., and each 7 in. wide.

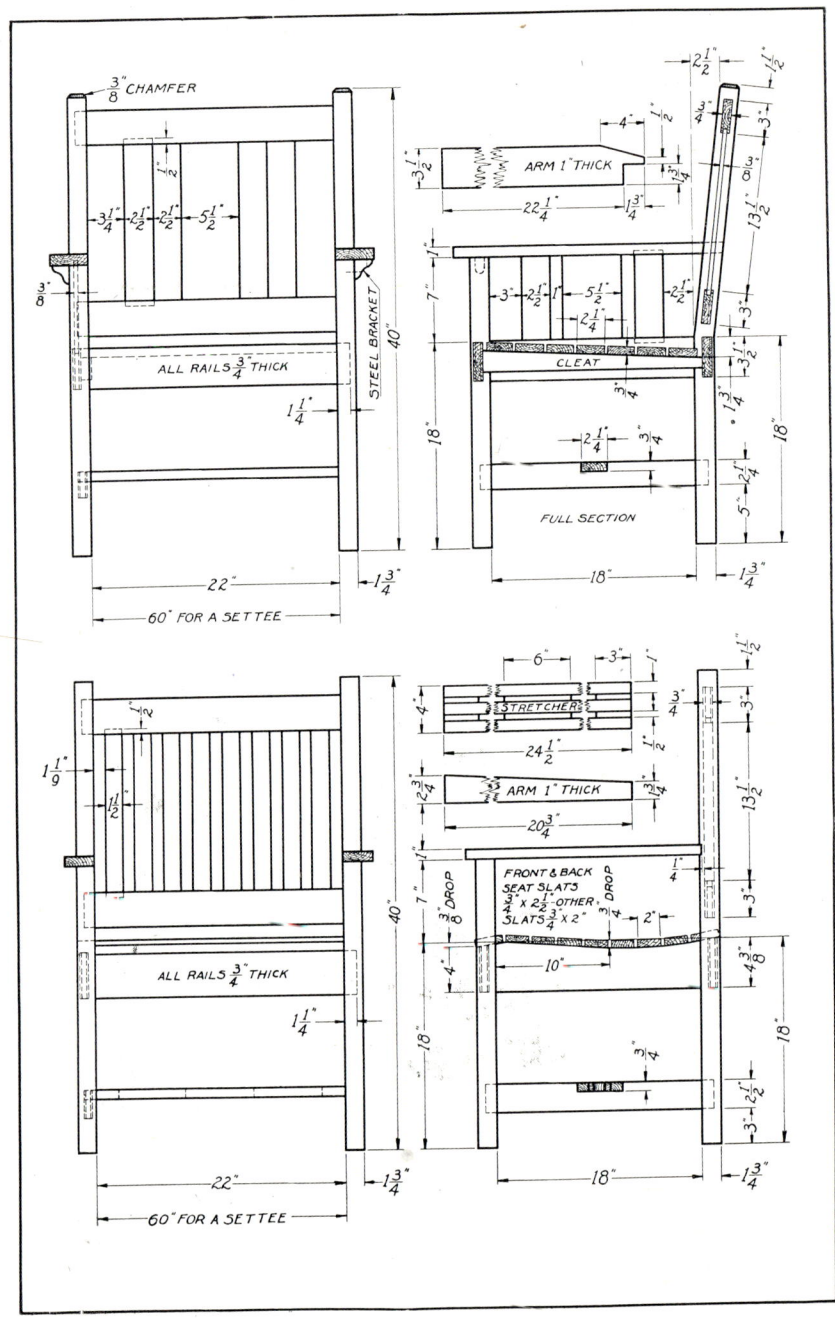

Fig. 6. Lawn or Porch Chairs and Settees

The bottom of the end pieces are then squared up and the pattern drawn. Before cutting to shape, the four mortises are to be laid out on each piece. They should be cut at least 1 in. deep by ½ in. wide. If shoulders are used on the edges of the tenons, they should not be made over 1/16 in., as it is desirable to have as wide a tenon as possible.

Full 1-in. stock should be used for the rails. Back slats should be ½ or ⅝ in. thick. One- or 1½-in. pieces of oak fastened to the ends with lag screws between the two bottom rails will give support to the seat slats and help to keep the ends from warping.

LAWN OR PORCH CHAIRS AND SETTEES

Although these designs call for many mortise-and-tenon joints, the finished product is worth the effort. They are dignified, light in weight, and strong if made with tight joints. The chairs in Figure 6 can be made to match the upper table in Figure 7.

Construction Details

The end view of the top chair is shown in "full section," that is, the chair is cut in half from front to back, the end view exposing the cut section. To make the back legs of this chair, the stock should be 4⅜ in. wide to allow for the slant. The seat slats fit between the end rails and are attached to and supported by two cleats which are fastened to the inside of the end rails with screws. The ends of these cleats must be notched out to fit over the inside corners of the legs. Why aren't the bottom slats placed on top of the end rails in this style?

Steel brackets are used to support the wide arm rests. The stretcher ends fit into the top of the lower rails for the full thickness of the stretcher. The rail tenons should be ⅜ in. thick and 1¼ in. deep. If shoulders are used on the edge of the tenons they should not be made over 1/16 in. They are not necessary as the side shoulder should suffice.

The stretcher in the bottom chair is built up of three 1-in. square pieces running full length. Between these 1-in. square pieces, there are two pieces ½ by 1 by 3 in. at each end, and two pieces ½ by 1 by 6 in. in the center. The ends of the stretcher are fastened to the bottom end rails in the same manner as the

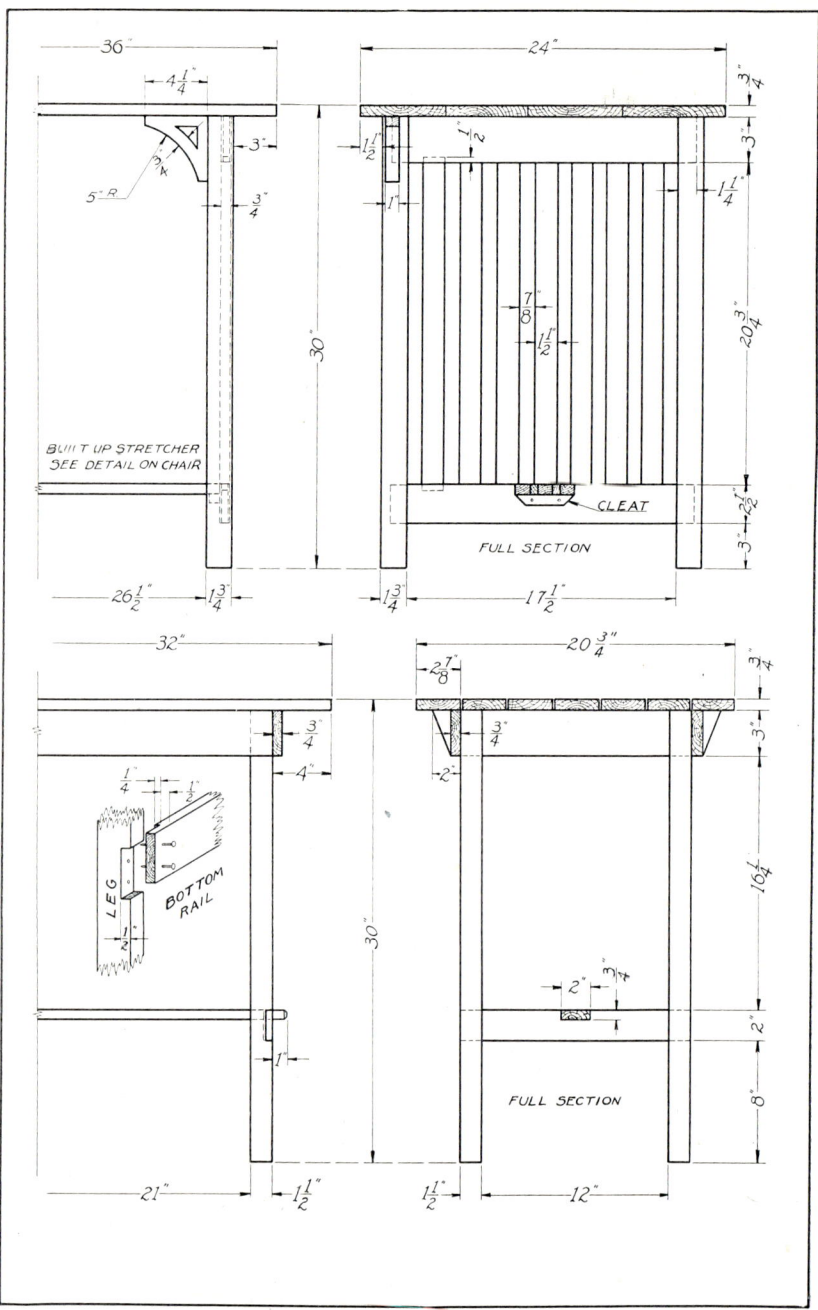

Fig. 7. Lawn or Porch Tables

one above. The end rails are shaped to form the curve of the seat slats. These slats project over the end rails flush with the outside of the legs. Thus they are 22 in. plus 1¾ in. plus 1¾ in. long for the chair and 60 in. plus 1¾ in. plus 1¾ in. for the settee. The rear of the horizontal arm fits into the back legs to the depth of ¼ in. Use the same size tenon as recommended for the chair above. Back slats are ¾ in. thick.

LAWN OR PORCH TABLES

The two tables shown in Figure 7 are very conservative. The upper one will match the lower chair in Figure 6. If the vertical slats and stretcher in this table are changed, it will also match the upper chair in Figure 6.

Construction Details

The unglued top shown on the bottom table is recommended for the lawn or garden, where there is no protection from the weather. If the table is intended for the porch the top may be glued. The end views of both tables are shown in "full section." The built-up stretcher is the same type as shown in Figure 6; however, the ends are fastened to the inside of the bottom rails with a cleat instead of being fitted into the top of the rail. The four brackets must be strongly fastened from underneath with flat-headed screws. The same size tenons as for the chairs in Figure 6 are recommended. The slats and rails are ¾ in.

The bottom table is simple to construct. The front and back rails are fastened on the outside of the legs as shown. The end rails overlap the front and back rails and extend beyond to support the outside top pieces. To strengthen the legs a ¼-in. shoulder is made on the bottom rails (see detail in Fig. 7). The stretcher projects 1 in. beyond the legs and has a 3/16-in. chamfer.

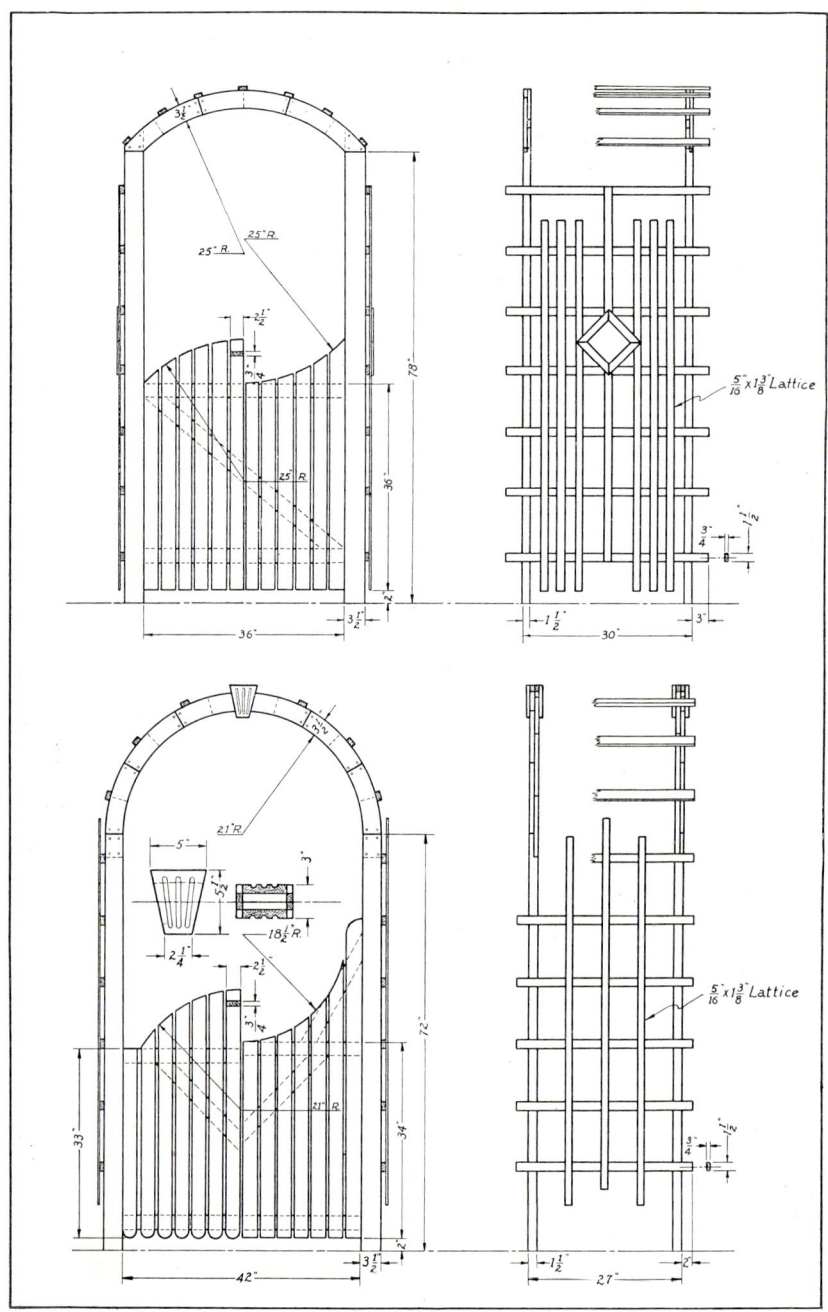

Fig. 8. Arched Gates

ARCHED GATES

The designs of the arched gates, fences, and garden seat in Figures 8, 9, 10, and 11, respectively, are related so that a number of combinations can be developed from them. The attractiveness of a well-designed arch will be greatly improved by a proper setting.

Construction Details

Both arches in Figure 8 are constructed from segments of ¾-in. softwood. In either case, two full-sized drawings of the arched portion should be drawn on building paper. One drawing may be cut into segment patterns and the other one cut to act as a template upon which to assemble the segments.

In the upper figure the four uprights should extend about 82 in. above the ground and at least 24 in. into the ground. Check your full-sized drawing to determine exactly how much of the upright is necessary to overlap one of the segments in the arch. Anchor posts may be used instead of letting the uprights go below the ground line, if desired. The method of using an anchor post is shown in Figure 14.

If a gate is desired, the top of it may be made to run parallel with the arch or just the reverse of it. The gate may best be made after the arch has been set into the ground. The horizontal crosspieces may be cut 40 in. long, and tacked to the wide surface of the uprights at the proper height. Thus the gate may be completed and then the horizontal pieces cut to length. This is a simple method for fitting the gate. The style and height of the gate should conform to the fence you have or intend to build.

In the bottom arch the fluted keystone is made of two ¾-in. pieces, 5 by 5½ in. (See cross section which shows upper half.) The flutes are ⅜ in. wide and half as deep. Tack each side of the keystone into position, one on each side of each arch, and fill in the spaces left with pieces cut to fit.

Eight-foot uprights are the most practical for this project; they allow 24 in. to fit below the surface. Anchor posts may be used if desired.

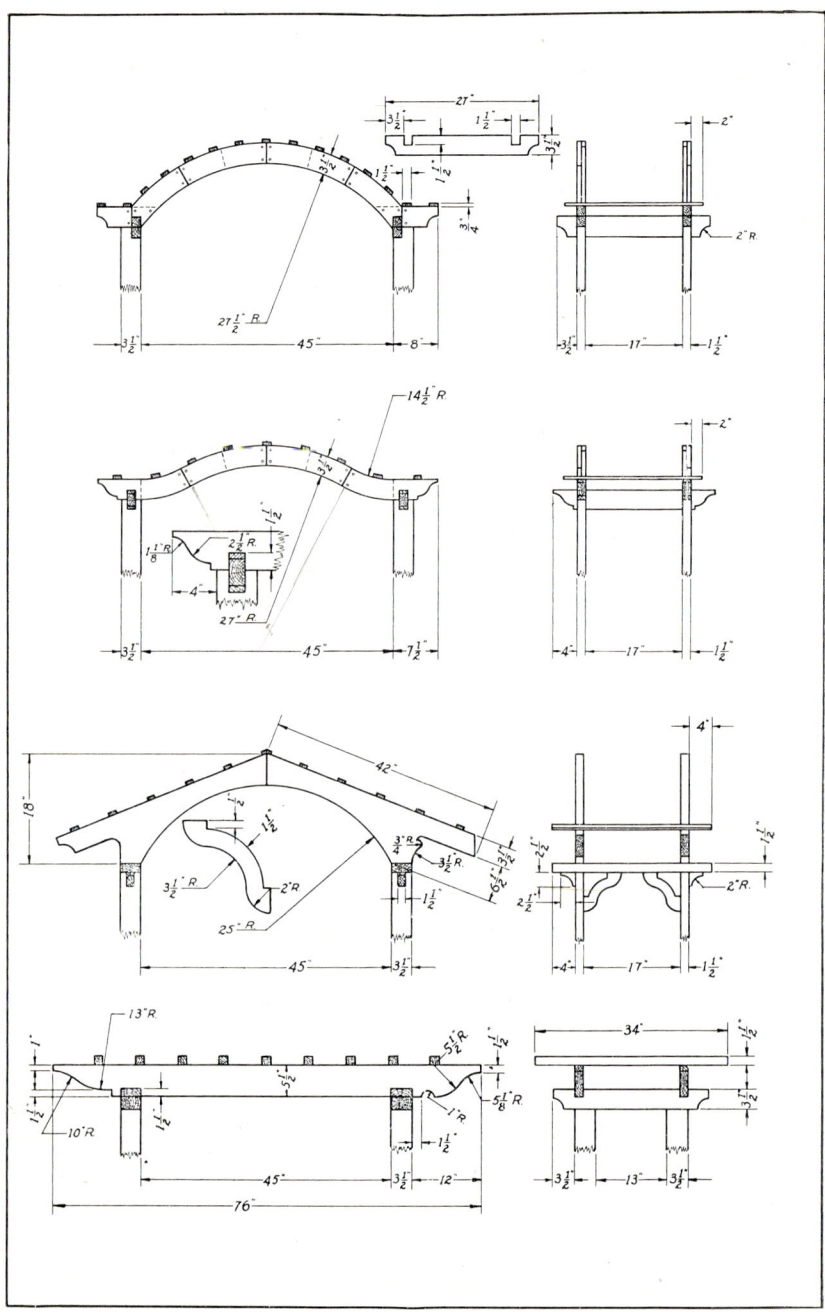

Fig. 9. Arches

ARCHES

Construction Details

To build either of the segmental curved arches see the "Construction Details" for Figure 8. The method of fastening these two arches to the uprights is interesting. In the first one, the horizontal crosspieces, each 27 in. long, are fastened to the underside of the arch with long screws, two at each joint, and driven from the underside. They are fastened to the uprights by long screws one at each joint and driven from the inside of the crosspieces to the uprights which have been notched out at these points to receive them. Several nails may be toenailed in each joint to keep the uprights from twisting.

An Arched Gate

In the second arch the horizontal crosspieces are constructed in the same manner. The uprights are notched out to receive them. Screws used in a similar manner to the above complete the fastening of the joints.

In the third arch either style rafter may be used. The horizontal crosspieces are fastened to the underside of the rafters. The uprights are toenailed to the crosspieces and further strengthened by the inside and outside brackets.

In the fourth arch either style of end cut on the cross rafter may be used. The $3\frac{1}{2}$-in. square horizontal cross bars are notched out to receive the cross rafters. Screws from the underside fasten the joints. The uprights are fastened to the cross

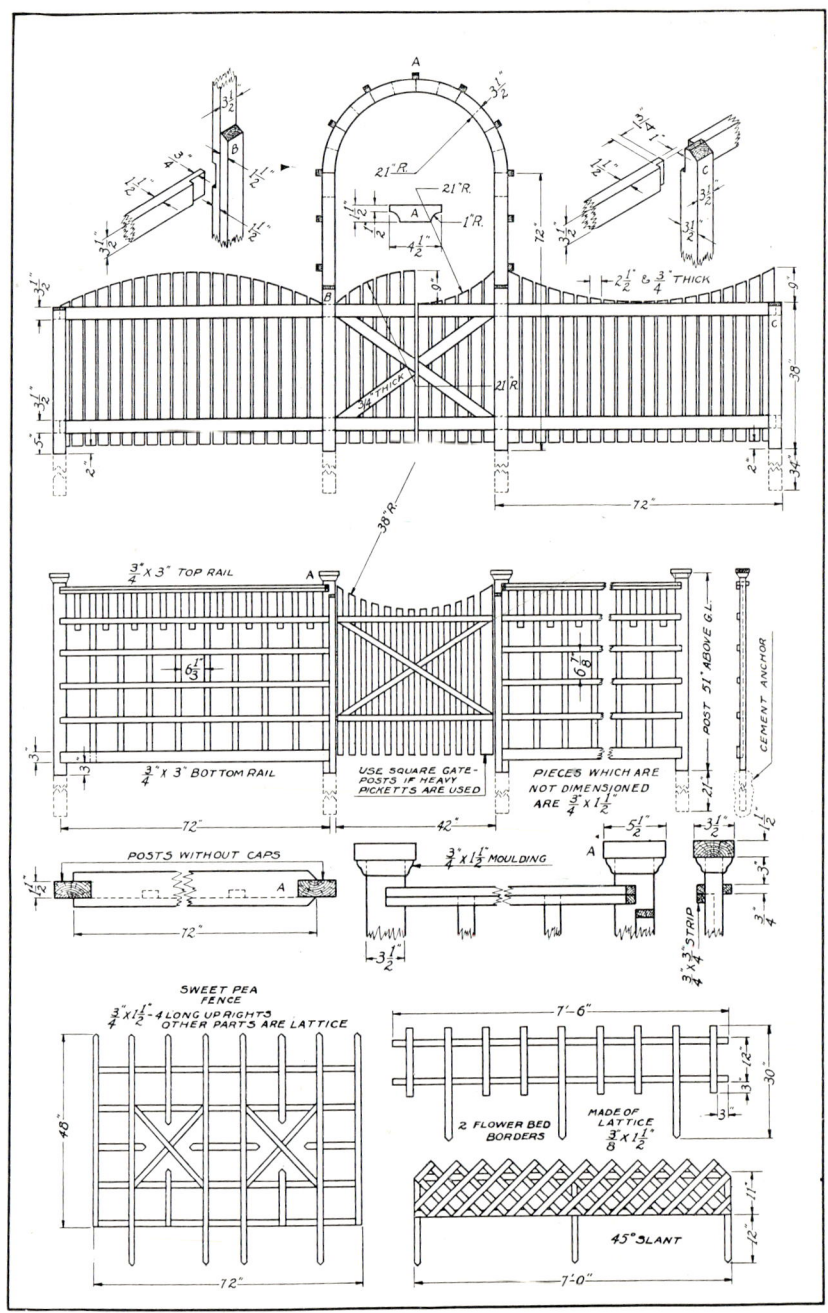

Fig. 10. Fences

bars by four long lag screws, one at each joint, which are screwed down from the top. The joints are then toenailed in order to complete the fastening. The decorative lattice work, height of uprights, and size of gates may be determined by the maker. Gate tops look well if they conform in shape to the arches or just the reverse (see Figs. 8 and 10).

FENCES

The "Construction Details" for the arched gates in Figure 8 will give an explanation for the construction of arch and gate illustrated.

Wood fences, painted white, have been popular since colonial times. They lend privacy and beauty to the home grounds and cut off the sight of alleys and unkept properties.

Constructing decorative fences on level ground is not difficult. Where the lot is irregular in surface some figuring is involved. In some cases the cross members which connect the posts are made parallel with the ground regardless of irregularity. Sometimes the cross members are made horizontal but placed at different levels. This gives a stairway effect. If the lot level has one direction of slope and does not vary over three feet in elevation, the cross members may be made horizontal with a low post on the high point and a high post on the low point. Obviously a 3-ft. fence on the high point will run to a 6-ft. fence on the low point if such a method is used. This is not objectionable in many cases. If the lot level does not vary over 5 ft., perhaps the angle formed by the ground line and the horizon can be split and that line should be followed with the cross members. In most cases the posts and slats will be kept vertical regardless of the position of cross members.

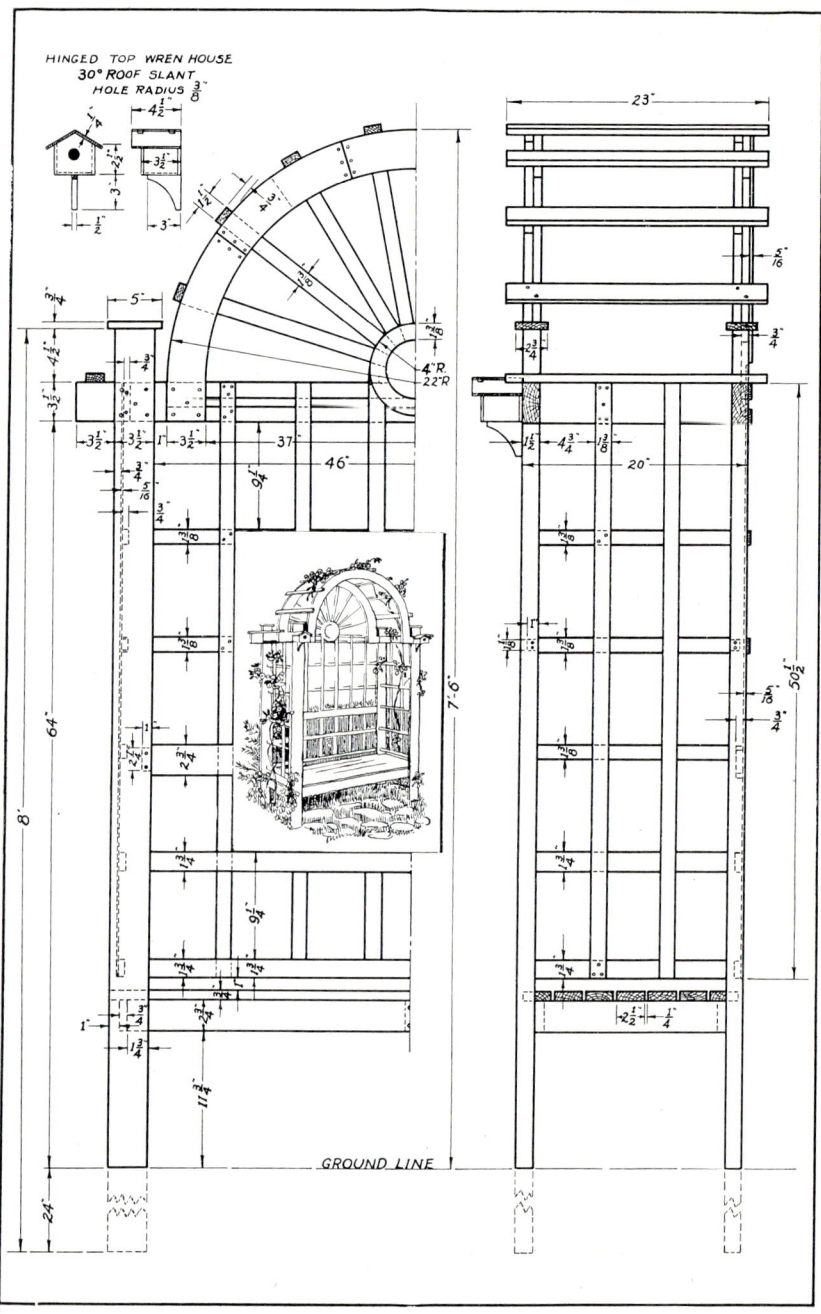

Fig. 11. Arched Garden Seat

ARCHED GARDEN SEAT

This arched seat is of a popular commercial design, and the dimensions have been reduced and the method of construction has been altered so as to fit the home tool chest. This garden seat has only six mortise-and-tenon joints.

Construction Details

The arched garden seat in Figure 11 is interesting because of the combinations which may be made from it. If the seat and back panel are omitted and the 64-in. dimension is changed to 74 in., it makes an excellent arched gateway. If the back panel is omitted it will still be attractive and seatable from either side.

To construct the segmental arch see the "Construction Details" of Figure 8. The uprights may be made of 6-ft. lengths if anchor posts are used (see Fig. 15) otherwise they should be 8 ft. These uprights are joined to the upper crosspieces with nailed cross-lap joints. The four upper crosspieces are joined to the arches in the same manner.

The 2¾-in. horizontal back slat is joined to the back uprights with nailed mortise-and-tenon joints. Glue is not necessary. The 1⅜-in. wide horizontal end slats, second from the top, are fastened in the same manner. The other horizontal and vertical slats are toenailed.

The front and back seat rails are nailed to the inside of the uprights. The end seat rails are nailed to the ends of the front and back rails. Triangular wooden blocks or angle irons are placed where the rails join to increase the strength of the joints.

The circular hub piece may be built of segments with overlapping joints or sawed from a solid board ¾ in. thick.

When nailing light lattice together, select a light nail that will protrude about ¼ in. so that the nail might be clinched. An iron should be held behind the pieces to lessen the shock on the lattice.

Place the bottoms of the two wren houses at the 64-in. elevation on the front uprights. To fasten, drive a screw through the back of the bird house from the inside. The screw driver will fit nicely through the hole. Fasten the bottom of the bird house to

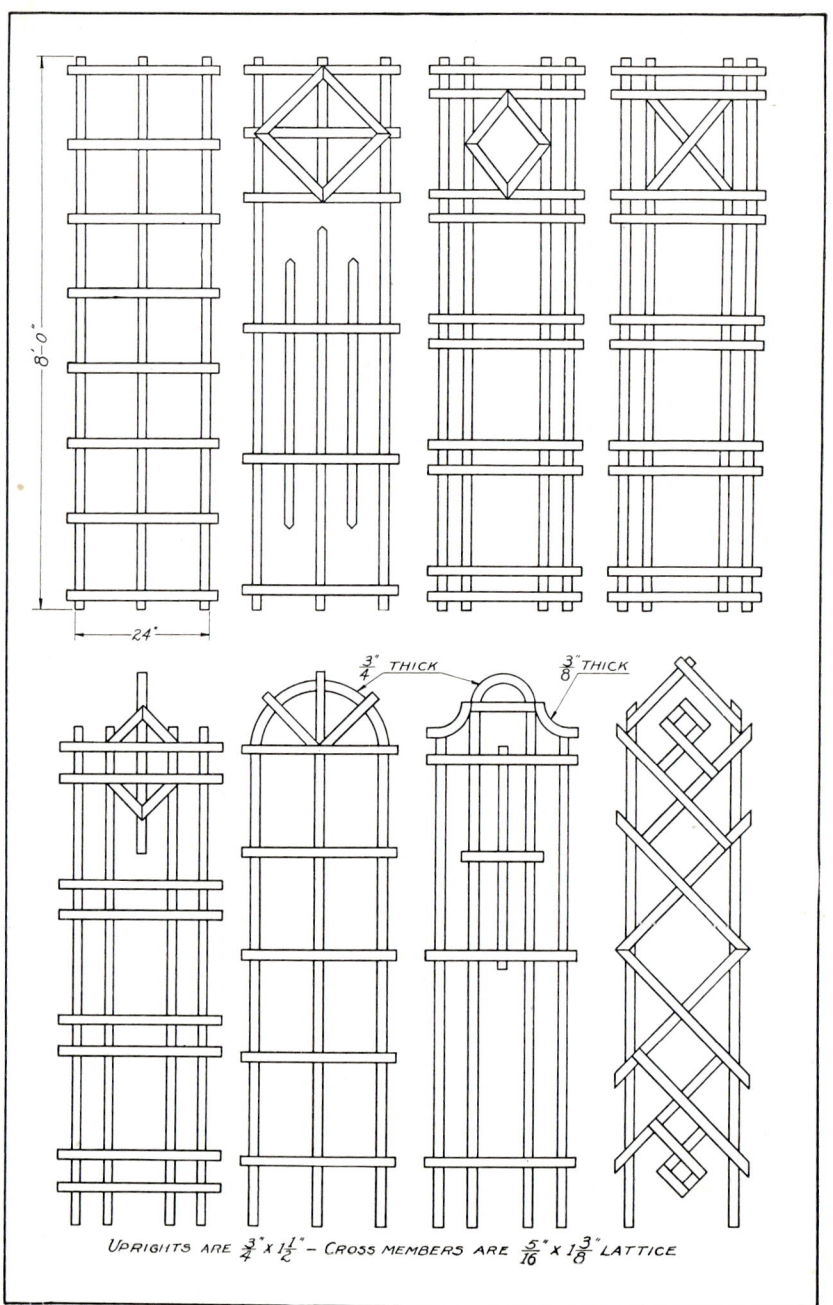

Fig. 12. Trellises

the bracket from the inside before attaching the roof. Then nail the bottom of the bracket to the upright.

TRELLISES

Just a few of the possibilities of trellis work are shown in Figures 12 and 13. Lattice material comes in various standard sizes and is obtainable in many lengths. Panels, such as illustrated, are inexpensive and suitable for many places: between windows, against fireplace chimneys, tree trunks, clothes posts, porch colonades, and so on. White is always an appropriate finish but green is attractive when placed in front of a contrasting color. Very often the top of the trellis is made similar to some architectural feature of the buildings on the grounds.

Construction Details

Only the over-all dimensions are given, as the proper spacing of the lattice can easily be determined from the illustrations. The uprights which run to the bottom are all ¾ by 1½ in. The curved top of the second trellis from the left on the bot-

A Trellis Used for a Climbing Bush

tom of Figure 12, is made of segments which connect behind the spokes. The topmost curve on the trellis next to it is made in one piece and is fastened to the back of the horizontal piece. The upper ends of the two convex curves are either cross-lapped with the horizontal piece or fastened to blocks which in turn are

[33]

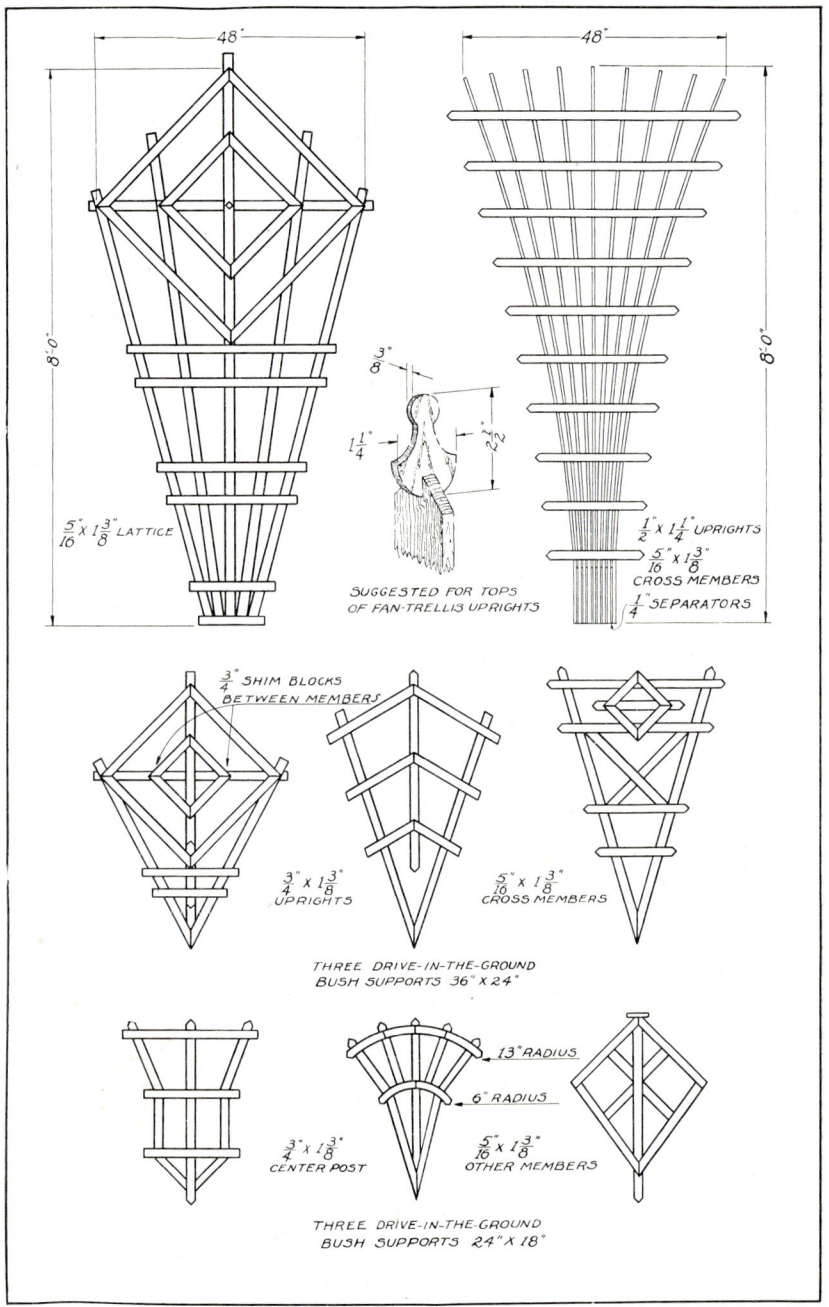

Fig. 13. Trellises

fastened to the outside of the two uprights and the ends of the concave piece.

TRELLISES

The creeping species of flowers are shown to best advantage when set off with an appropriate background. The baby rambler needs a large trellis with considerable spread to best exhibit its beauty, and dwarfed variety of rose cannot be expected to grow to the top of an 8-ft. trellis. Although well-designed trellises attract a great deal of attention, they are made for flowers and vines to creep on and thus have to be built according to the vine they are intended for.

Construction Details

The upper trellises are suitable for varieties of large creepers. The one at the left is made entirely from 5/16 by 1 3/8-in. lattice, so it is not stiff enough to stand supported by an anchor post alone. Fan trellises are rigid and need only an anchor post for support. If the uprights and separators are fastened by two long bolts, this portion is strong enough to be fastened to an anchor post. The fan trellis illustrated looks complete without the suggested top designs but some may prefer these added decorations. Notches may be cut into the uprights or into the added pieces.

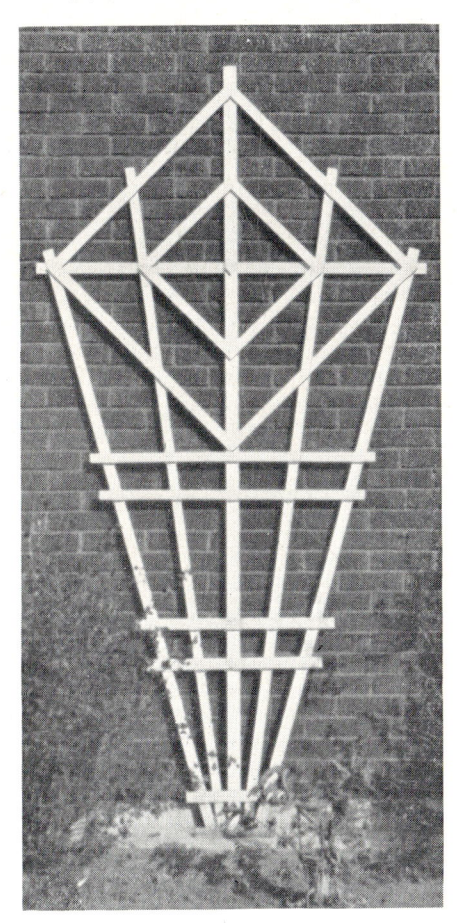

A Trellis Helps to Offset a Blank Wall

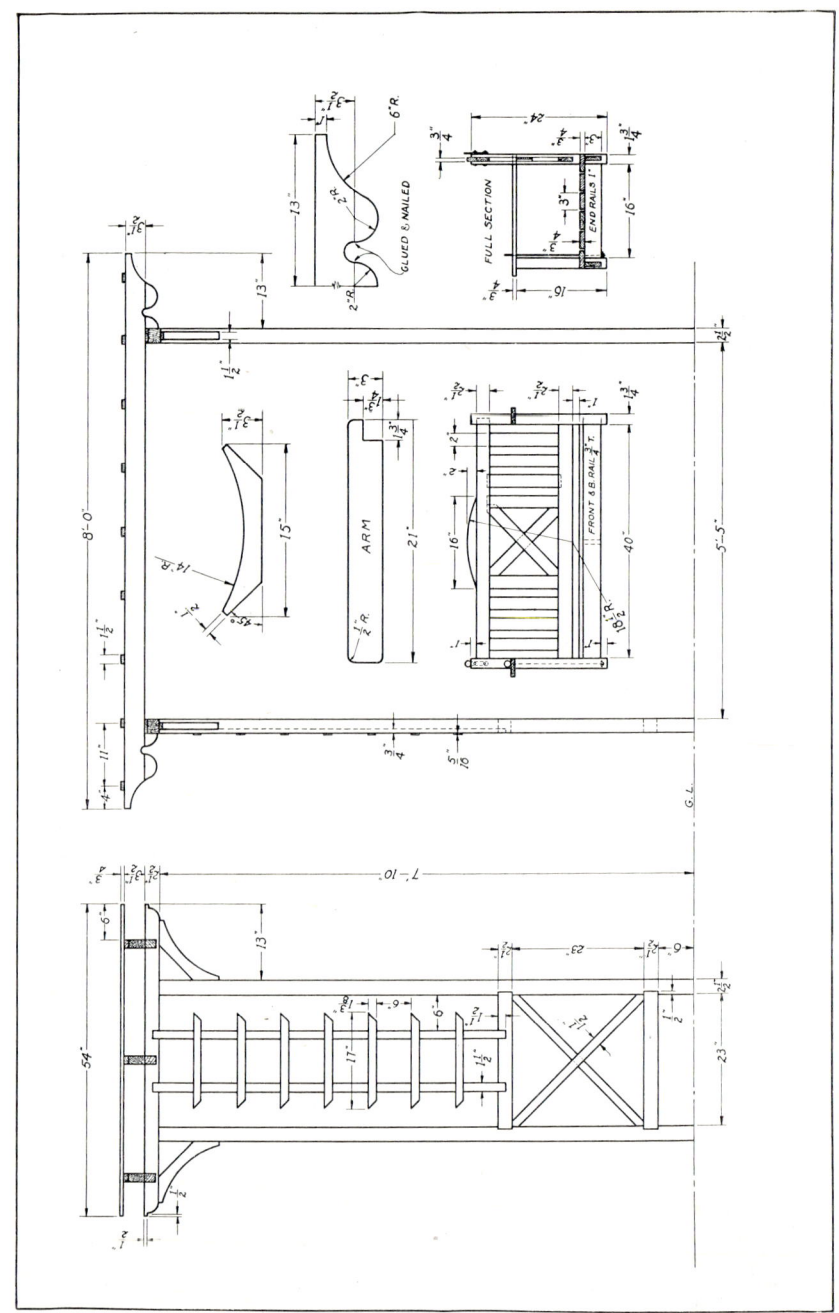

Fig. 14. Junior Pergola Swing

The lower trellises are supported by the ground alone but anchor posts may be needed in light soils. The large upper left-hand trellis matches the small trellis in the center row at the left.

JUNIOR PERGOLA SWING

The size of this swing proves more popular for the average home grounds and the cost is considerably less than the swing shown in Figure 15. Some care should be taken about placing the swing on the grounds with regard to shade and privacy.

Construction Details

If there is not enough room in the school or home shop, because of too many large projects being built at the same time or lack of space, the pergola parts can be assembled outside. The decorative undercurves on the ends of the cross rafters should be fastened with waterproof casein glue and then nailed. The uprights of the trellises are made of ¾-in. stock and set into the horizontal pieces. A cross-lap joint is used at the center of the pieces that cross between the bottom bracing. These horizontal bottom braces are 2½ in. wide. They should fit tight because they keep the uprights stiff and prevent rocking. Lag screws and washers are used for fastening wherever possible.

The long rail tenons on the swing are ⅜ in. by 1¼ in. The short or end-rail tenons are ½ by 1¼ in. The crosspieces in the back are cross-lapped at the center. The tenons are marked out for these pieces after the cross lap has been made and the swing back temporarily assembled. Lay the cross-lapped pieces into position from the far side of the back and mark the shoulders of the tenons at the four inside corners formed by the back rails and slats. The curved top piece is either nailed or nailed and glued to the top rail.

The iron fixtures for the chains on the back posts are bolted on the rear side of the posts. The front fixtures are rods with eyes at the top and threads at the bottom. They pass down through the arms right behind the front posts and through the end rails where they are held by nuts. The fixtures on the pergola are either heavy screw eyes or bands of iron which fit around the center cross rafter. See the anchor post in Figure 15.

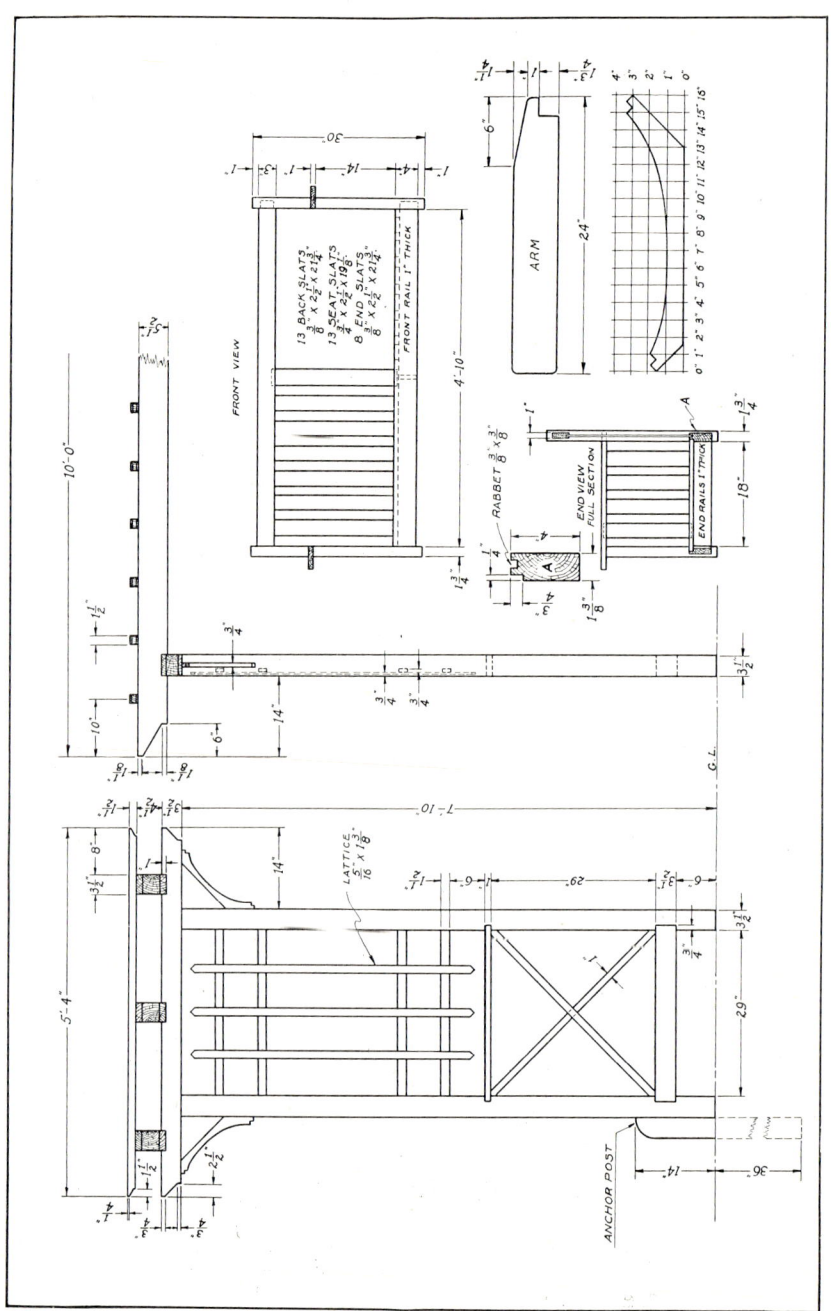

Fig. 15. Senior Pergola Swing

SENIOR PERGOLA SWING

This swing is designed so that it can be used on large grounds, golf courses, and in parks.

Construction Details

The uprights are 8 ft. long and are fastened with bolts or lag screws to anchor posts at the ground line. The horizontal pieces of the trellises fit into the ¾ by 1½-in. mortises. Cross-lap joints are used at the juncture of the cross braces. These cross braces

Senior Pergola Swing

are 3½ in. wide and must fit tight at the ends. Lag screws and washers are used to fasten the heavy members together.

The swing is simple in construction. The rail tenons are ½ by 1¼ in. The back rail is 1⅜ in. thick as shown at A in Figure 15. A ¼-in. shoulder is made in the front and back rail to support the seat slats which run from the front to back. A ⅜ by ⅜ in. rabbet may be made in the back and end rails to receive the vertical slats. If this method is used instead of mortises then

[39]

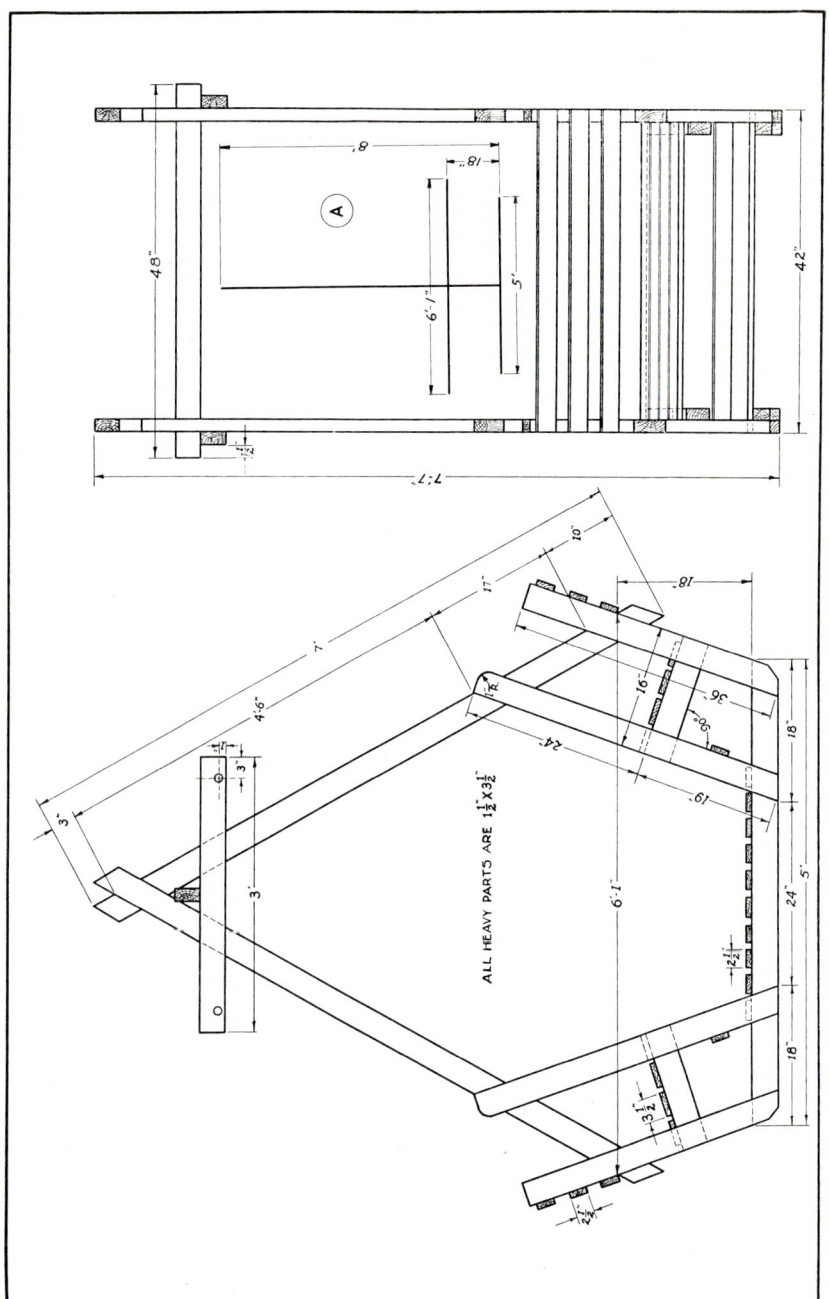

Fig. 16. Swing

strips of wood ⅜ by ⅜ in. must be tacked into the rabbets between the slats to separate them. The same method or mortises should be used under the arms. The "Construction Details" for Figure 14 will show how to attach the chain fixtures.

SWING

This comfortable swing is easy to make. When suspended from a high crossbar between two trees it sways in the lightest breeze with a gentle rocking motion, making it adaptable to the summer cottage.

Construction Details

The framework is made from 2 by 4's which are dressed down to 1½ by 3½ in. Cross-lap joints are used on the 7-ft. pieces at all points where other members contact them except at the two top outside crossbars and the top stretcher crossbar. The other joints of the frame are made by nailing together the full thickness of the pieces with the exception of the top stretcher bar. Vertical and horizontal cuts are made in the 7-ft. pieces to admit the full size of the stretcher bar. The tread, seat and back slats, and foot rests for children are nailed on the places indicated.

To lay out the swing (see diagram A, Fig. 16) draw a straight chalk line on the floor 5 ft. long and bisect it. From the bisection start a second line making this 8 ft. long and at right angles to line one. On this 8-ft. line lay off a point 18 in. from the first line. Through

Swing Suspended from a High Limb

[41]

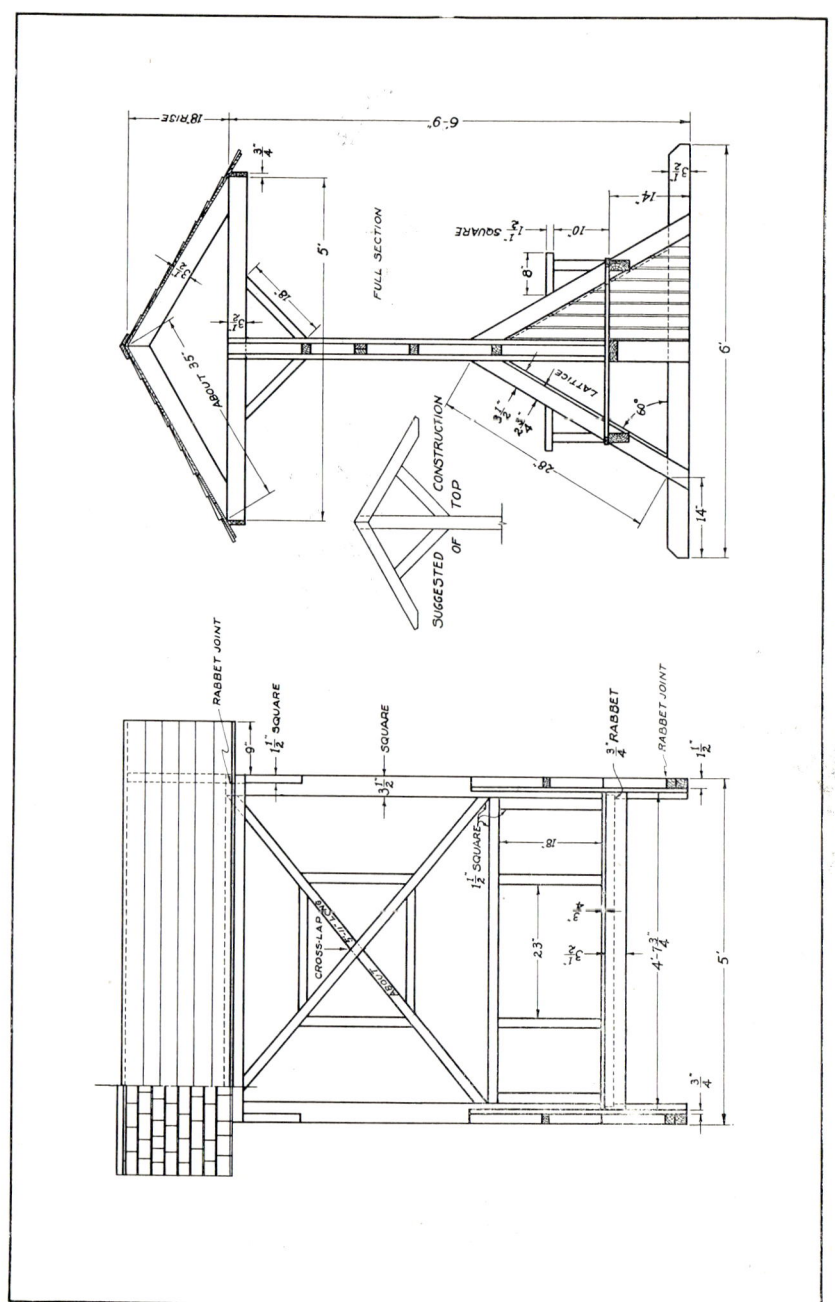

Fig. 17. Canopied Double Seat

this point draw a line 6 ft. 1 in. long, parallel to the 5-ft. line, and bisected by the 8-ft. line. Now lay a piece of 2 by 4, 5 ft. long, face down so that one top edge falls on line one. This piece is one of the two bottom supports on which the treads are later to be nailed. Then the 7-ft. pieces are laid on the floor in the proper relation to the 5-ft. piece and the lines. Next, the two 36-in. pieces and then the two 43-in. pieces are placed in position. The layout should be checked for accuracy and then the joints marked and numbered. The cross laps are now cut and assembled. The second set of 2 by 4's may be laid out in the same manner or on the set already assembled.

CANOPIED DOUBLE SEAT

The seat illustrated in Figure 17 has been improved in a few of the details from the standpoint of construction over the seat in the frontispiece. This type of seat may well be used on golf courses, at summer cottages, in parks, and so forth, as well as on the home grounds. An entrance gate with the same type of top will harmonize with it. This seat is very attractive when finished white and with dark-green shingles.

Construction Details

The end view is shown in full section in order to illustrate the construction more clearly. The 3½-in. square uprights are rabbeted in three places: at the tops and bottoms to receive the cross members, on the outside, and under the seat slats on the inside to receive the center cross brace. The four 28-in. braces are dressed 2 by 4's, the bottoms of which are nailed on the top edges of the two 6-ft. bottom 2 by 4's. Along the inside of these four 28-in. braces and nailed to them are four ¾ by 2¾-in. pieces which extend to the ground. Thus ¾ by 1-in. shoulders are formed against which the lattice slats are nailed. The arm rests and supports are nailed on the 28-in. braces as shown.

The parts to be assembled last are the cross supports. Lay these pieces at their right slant on the far side of the 3½-in. square uprights and mark the angles. Be sure that the uprights are vertical before doing so. A cross-lap joint is made at their juncture. The angles on the two horizontal pieces, one above

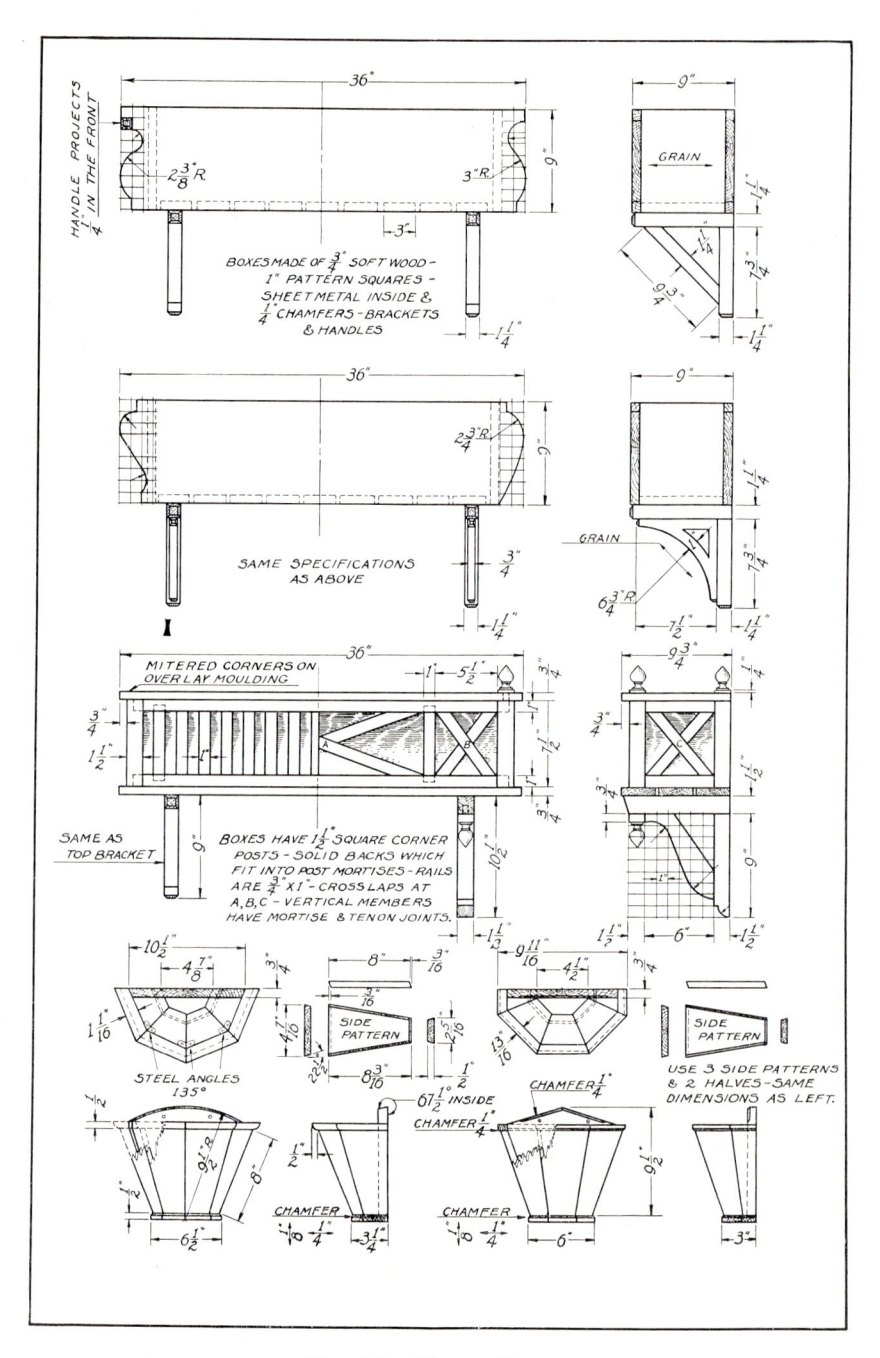

Fig. 18. Flower Boxes

and one below the cross-lap joints, are marked from the angles formed by the long cross pieces and the horizontal back rest. How would you mark the angles on the remaining two vertical pieces? Bolts and lag screws should be used wherever possible. Anchor posts may be used if necessary.

FLOWER BOXES

Flower boxes designed with care and properly placed add to the beauty of any home grounds. They usually are paired to balance the effect. Boxes placed beneath windows are easily maintained. The basket type of flower box may be used to advantage on the sides of an entrance.

Construction Details

The three upper illustrations show one half of six different boxes and end views of the three designs. The four upper boxes vary only in the designs on their fronts and sides, the construction and dimensions being the same. Two designs of brackets are shown. All of the boxes should be metal lined. It is not necessary to cut holes in the bottom of the containers.

The third illustration from the top in Figure 18 shows two boxes of similar construction. The rails in each are $3/4$ in. thick and the rail tenons are $3/8$ by 1 by 1 in. The end of the box at the left, though not shown, has three vertical slats spaced slightly closer together than the front slats. All slats are $3/4$ in. thick, the sides of which are flush with the sides of the rails. The rails are offset $1/8$ in. from the posts on the outside. The inside of the overlay molding is flush with the inside of the rails.

The two basket boxes are both semioctagonal in shape. The one at the left is as wide as the length of the major axis of the full octagon, and the one at the right is as wide as the length of the minor axis of the same size octagon; therefore the side patterns are of the same size but the left-hand one has four full-sized sidepieces and the right-hand one has three full-sized sidepieces and two half-sized sidepieces. The sidepieces are fastened at the top with metal angles on the inside. Overlay moldings are tacked on at the tops. The bottoms are nailed from below. Semicircular or semioctagonal metal containers should be used.